Presence and Potential

Experience Your Higher Self and Live in Wholeness

Martha Creek

Contents

Author's Note

Welcome to *Presence and Potential, Experience Your Higher Self and Live in Wholeness.* This book is for ALL people with desire to increase their leadership and lower anxiety; whether you are a parent, president, or person in leadership. The terms used here lean toward leadership and the truth is, if you have this book in your hand, you are undoubtedly leading a family, relational dynamics in groups, churches, offices, workspaces, neighborhoods or corporations. If you are looking for a practical approach to the most common humanity dynamics, keep reading. If you want to be better at regulating yourself, keeping a clear distinction between facts and feelings, and staying empowered in tense situations of any flavor, this writing is for you.

As we learn how to do leadership differently, in all areas of life, we create a very new way of being with self and others. In this book, I use leadership materials based on the learning throughout my lifetime from various sources, including Healthy Congregations, Inc., an organization whose focus is around growing thoughtful leaders. You can find out more at healthycongregations.com.

A congregation, though commonly referred to as a spiritual group, is actually any group that is interacting and united in a common purpose, including relationships and families.

I invite you to open your mind to consider how you're relating, leading, developing, modeling behaviors of all kinds and please avoid any shame, blame, and self-hate. As we look at ourselves honestly, some of our unhelpful patterns will be revealed. As we accept our own humanity about this, we can learn from our past. We can learn from the unhealthy patterns we picked up in our families of origin. We can see clearly how those patterns are still prominent today.

The tools in this book will help you become a better leader in your family, your neighborhood, your organizations, and yes, in your congregation. I offer this book in the context of leadership in general, with a heartfelt thanks to Healthy Congregations for the basis of this material.

—Martha Creek

Testimonials

"Martha's down home, bottom line, 'what is, is' way of being is a teacher to us all. Martha doesn't just own the knowledge, she is the knowledge!" —Janet Bray Attwood, Co-Author of New York Times Bestseller, *The Passion Test*

"Martha has the innate ability to hold your heart and sometimes your hand as she leads you back to yourself- your own wisdom, your own integrity." —Diane Czerwonka, A life forever changed.

"Martha is a well-known teacher, trainer and facilitator. She serves by modeling authenticity. Her works provides basic truths that are beneficial not only in your spiritual community's leadership, but also in your personal life. I am a better minister, spiritual leader, partner, mother, daughter and friend because of my connection to Martha Creek and her teachings." —Denise Yeargin, Retired Unity Minister

Testimonials

"There are few people in my life, that when I meet them, I have an instant recognition of authenticity, depth of knowing and pure love. I call these people 'the real deal.' Martha is the real deal. If you have the opportunity to be in her orbit, I heartfully encourage you to give yourself the gift of Martha. Big love." —Rev. Jude Denning, Senior Minister, Unity of Stuart, FL

"Martha's embracing yet confronting spirit has brought deep inner growth and a greater bond of mutual respect and love for our organization and teams." —Rev. Chris Jackson, Senior Minister, Unity on the Bay - Miami, FL

"Rev. Martha Creek has created a beautiful mark on my being. She has taught me how to focus my thoughts, to simplify and yet evaluate with depth and honest appraisal the inner messages being sent my way. She encourages love in all forms and the exploration of a well lived life, facing every fear, turning every corner, and by all means, celebrating every moment." —Noell Rowan, PhD, Wilmington, NC

"Next to God, Martha Creek may be the wisest, most wonderful teacher on the planet. I turn cartwheels in gratitude that our paths crossed. Thank you, Martha, for well, everything!!!" —Pam Grout, #1 New York Times bestselling author of 19 books

Find more Testimonials at
https://www.marthacreek.com/every-testimonial-in-a-list/.

Introduction

The tenets of *Presence and Potential* are simple, but not easy. Putting these leadership qualities into practice can take a lifetime to master. I know, because even after decades of teaching and living this material, I still find places within me where I catch myself off guard. I suddenly find myself practicing a lower-consciousness, "knee jerk" response to a situation. I find myself having to be mindful to live into the raised-up, empowering response that brings me greater connection with others and greater peace within myself.

Make no mistake, this is deep inner work. And this deep work, also known as The Greatest Adventure, is filled with curiosity and wonder at the power we each have to create a fuller and satisfying life, a life where we are present to the now and at our highest emotional level. I invite you to join me on this adventure for yourself!

Chapter 1
Define Yourself to Others And Stay Connected to Them

As we begin, I want you to imagine your life if you were actually doing each of these exercises offered throughout these pages. My invitation is for embodiment of the practices, not just in theory.

How do we define ourselves to others *and* stay connected to them? This is the first key to unlocking your authentic leadership skills. How can I say, "Well, this is what I'm thinking and believing, and I'm just as open to hearing what you think and believe about the topic. Not only am I open to it, I'm willing to change my mind so that I *could* learn something from you. Not that I *would* necessarily change my mind, but I'm open to consider the possibility. I could get a piece of information from you, or learn something from you, that could actually shift where I stand."

The key difference in this shift is that it doesn't come from an emotional response. It's not a knee-jerk reaction to what another person says. It's not coming from a reaction of "You'll be mad at me," or "You're going to hold this against me," if you don't agree with the other person. The shift comes more from having an open mind to what the other person is sharing; to reach a point where you can truly say, "This makes sense to me. I *have* learned something here that would cause me to change my mind."

How can you be clear about where you stand based on your own convictions and be as open and as accepting and as understanding to another and where that person stands on a matter?

On the surface, with most conversations, this may sound easy to do. But what about harder conversations? Imagine you're at your next family gathering and someone in your family brings up their political views, their religious views, or any views they hold that you disagree with.

What would it be like if you were *actually* open to hear where they stand on a matter? Use the opportunity to speak in terms of, "Well, this is what I think and this is what I believe, *and* I honor and understand where you stand, what *you* think and what *you* believe. I'm just as interested in understanding where you're coming from as I am wanting you to understand where I'm coming from."

There's such power in defining yourself in ways that allow you to stay connected with others. And please don't believe me until you've applied this technique for yourself —without applying these techniques in your life, it's just me blathering about it.

There are many stories in my family about me not believing the way the rest of the family believes. In most of these stories, I gave up myself in order to not ruffle their feathers. I did what I thought needed to be done to keep peace at any price. This did not serve me well over time because I didn't have any authentic *self.* I wasn't honoring myself.

On the surface it looked like I was gaining a sense of self by keeping the peace, but it was really more of a pseudo-self. I wasn't gaining *anything.* In fact, when we do this, we eventually lose something – it all begins to build up a patterned response. Giving away self leads to hurts and transgressions, keeping score and building resentments, and all the other things that erode relationships, erodes peace of mind and everything else of value to us.

Today, I work to define myself and let others have their own perspectives, including political beliefs. I don't have to insert my opinion and preferences around political matters when my family is in discussion about politics. If they're not asking me about where I stand or what I believe, then I take that as an indicator they're not all that interested in my beliefs, and that's actually okay.

This is a much healthier approach for me than the extreme of withholding what I actually think and believe because I don't want to cause others to react in anger, or get hurt or upset, or engage in some kind of right versus wrong conversation over it. Over time, not feeling the need to exercise or insert my opinion has saved me much angst.

Another example of defining myself and staying connected to others includes my ordination path. From the very beginning, I looked at how I was going to serve ministries; not taking a traditional role of ministering. I never intended to go out and lead churches. My calling was to minister to minsters and to serve those who serve – and that required a non-traditional approach.

I didn't plan to take a non-traditional path to ordination; and I've taken a lot of heat about that over time. I've been challenged, called names, estranged and excluded from groups and gatherings. In certain settings, I was not allowed to use the title "Reverend" when my ordination was from an ordination path different from the denomination where I was going to speak.

I didn't mind that. I understood where they were coming from. I understood what their standards were regarding ordination. *And*, I wasn't going to let their position stop me from continuing on my path.

I was able to define myself. I'm fine if I use the title Reverend; I'm fine if I don't. I don't justify my title or explain how I got it or how my credentials are as valid as anyone else's.

Another example of that is traditional college. My friends were going to college the standard way, moving away to attend college. I could see that's a viable path for going to college, *and* it wasn't my path. I never intended to head off for four years to get my education.

I completed all the high-school courses they offered toward college degrees at the closest university to where I lived, which was Western Kentucky University. At night after high school, I took college classes while working three jobs. There I was, with a full-time job and two part-time jobs—and going to college full time. I did it *my* way. I didn't have to do it the traditional way in order to stay connected to friends who were taking a more traditional route. I didn't have to make their route right or wrong and I didn't have to promote my way. I understood my way was right for me and not necessarily right for anybody else.

Learn how to define yourself – and stay in touch with others, stay open to what they're thinking, what they're believing, what the basis of their beliefs are – while having a firm foundation of your own beliefs. Not feeling the need to change your own convictions out of emotional reactivity to others. Staying open-minded enough to consider "I may actually learn something from this other person's beliefs." You would be well-served indeed to soften your views or to look again at what you believe. Defining yourself to others and staying connected to others allows you to clarify your beliefs. And to even have a willingness to change your mind if this new belief is true for you and not simply an emotional reaction to someone else's beliefs.

Chapter 2
Regulate Your Own Anxiety

Regulating your own anxiety starts with being able to put the oxygen mask on yourself first. You've heard that airplane announcement about what to do with the falling oxygen masks if the cabin suddenly loses pressure, right? Before you can help another person, you need to put your own oxygen mask on first. Before you or I can help another person, in any situation that evokes anxiety, we need to regulate our own anxiety first. That's why – on emergency room walls – on the chart of actions first responders should do first, step one is to "regulate your own pulse."

Before we can help another human being or bring any calm, clarity, or coherency to a situation, it's necessary for us to regulate our own anxiety.

Regulating anxiety sounds easy, and yet it is one of the most difficult tools I've practiced throughout my life. After decades of practicing this, how struck I am when I see very mature, intelligent, highly functioning people (including myself at times) unable to regulate anxiety or not able to do this systematically, or in a broader spectrum of experiences and situations.

I remember the first time I was able to do this. I was a young girl, and my uncle and I were in a farm accident. My uncle and I were riding in a wagon, being pulled by a tractor. The tractor hit a tree and my uncle was jarred off the wagon and was injured. Somehow, I was able to stay calm. I got off the wagon, situated him on the ground, began directing my family—even though I was a child —"You go get the car, you help me pick him up. Now we carry him over to the road so he can be driven to the hospital."

A calmness in me caused me to be able to think, organize and strategize about what would be a series of sane, sensible actions to get him off that farmland and onto the road where he could be driven in a car to an emergency room.

I reflect on that quite a bit and how that calmness was in me at a very early age. I also remember being at funerals where there was a great deal of emotion being expressed – wailing and praying and crying and shrieking. I had the capacity to hold space for people experiencing a grief process of intense loss. I was able to keep myself calm, and to regulate my own emotions and feelings so I could be of support emotionally and spiritually for other people who were buried in loss and grief. We all can learn to regulate anxiety in high-stress situations, without denying our own feelings and losses.

We have been taught many common and profound practices to regulate anxiety, such as pausing before responding, or pausing before proceeding. I'm fond of phrasing this practice as "The Three P's." I've been known to say "pause, pray, and proceed" or "pause, presence, then proceed" or "pause, prepare, and then proceed." Find whatever your Three P's are. Application is the key, of course.

This tool has served me well in every profession I've had, including human resources, ministry, coaching, counseling, family matters, and relationship matters. Pausing, preparing, and then proceeding will serve you well. In regulating our own feelings, anxiety, and thoughts, we become informed, aligned, and connected. This practice makes us collaborative, innovative, thoughtful listeners, and strong space-holders for others.

Think about this concept in terms of animals. Our behavior under stress closely mimics animal behavior. Look at a herd of cattle in a field surrounded by an electric fence. When one cow touches the fence, it gets shocked, is startled, and it starts to stampede.

It's running to get away from the enemy, the electric fence. Without thinking, without any cause in reality, the entire herd will stampede after this one cow. They did not experience shock. They were not hurt. There was no enemy to them. But they reacted as if there were. We often do the same thing. Because of our own herd mentality, we also will herd, in effect.

How do we change this reaction? By taking a moment to pause and become, in essence, a "circuit breaker."

When someone else is panicked, angry, or upset, we often run away from a situation without pausing to think, pausing to see if there is any real threat in the field. Is there a reason to be running or stampeding or leaving a scene? Without that pause, we live from a regressed state. We're living in the animalistic brain, the reptilian brain—

the teeny little part of our brain that only has a repertoire of three options: fight, flight, or freeze. In this example, we'd be reacting to our flight mechanism.

So the question is not *do I do this?* Of course, you do. We all do. It's instinctual, hardwired, automatic. When it happens, it can even seem like we don't have any control over it. It's such a knee-jerk reaction and such a patterned response that we feel unable to control ourselves. We take action without even knowing what we are doing.

This is what we're dealing with here; a power of a reaction that is so innate, so instinctual, so automatic. Saying "regulate my own anxiety" is no little thing. To be able to build in a pause when we get triggered, when we get upset, affronted, afraid, panicked, terrorized, humiliated, embarrassed—any such emotion that arises. Our task is to create an automatic pause in the situation, in our reaction.

So before we speak, pause. Before we defend, pause. Before we go to war with another, pause. Before we go silent or withhold—whatever our patterned ways of being are—we put the pause in there first.

How can we get calmer? Take a deep breath. Count to three. Remember, the person before us is a human being. The "enemy" in front of us may actually be someone we deeply care about. All the more reason to stay coherent and be more present to the field before we stampede.

Decide for yourself, what are ways you can regulate your own anxiety? How can you be calm even when other people are not? How can you be a calming influence in a herd mentality? When others would stampede or run the other way, how can you be a calmer, less anxious presence in situations? Whatever the situation in your life, your workplace, your family, with your children, your spouse, or other close relationship. How can you be a "circuit breaker" for anxiety? Instead of joining in, commiserating, colluding, herding with others, examine how you can be a circuit breaker instead. Imagine what it would be like if you could employ this tool of regulating your anxiety once you have some practice at being that circuit breaker.

As we continue through these twenty-six tools, use just one of them tools when you find yourself in a sticky situation. Implementing just one new skill in the "now" moment increases your ability to be present *and* makes you higher functioning. It changes the entire reality of the situation. It changes the whole scene. It changes your experience of your life. It changes the relational dynamics, and makes for a lot easier and happier life.

Chapter 3
Keep a Clear Distinction
Between Facts and Feelings

The facts. What *are* the facts? What are the *feelings* about the facts? The *facts* are, there was a snake. The *feelings* about "there was a snake" may be panic, terror, worry, upset—the "I've got to get out of here" desire to flee.

Our feelings and our emotions are all effects of the thought that, "I'm not safe. I'm in danger here." Think about the effects of similar feelings.

To practice and apply this clear distinction between facts and feelings, especially in particularly intense situations, takes practice. How do we learn to tell the difference between facts and feelings?

Imagine hearing a comment again and again like, "I'm broke, I'm broke, I'm broke." This is *feeling* based. The truth could be "I have a minus-$13 bank balance, or I have $3 in the bank." This is *factual*.

How do you make this distinction between facts and feelings in your own life?

Maybe you ask someone to dinner and they say "no" to you. Your mind will make up that their "no" means "I'm not valuable, I'm not important, I'm not a priority. They don't care about me, I'm not safe with them."

Our minds go off and interpret all manner of things, giving layers of meaning to what "actually-factually" happened. We won't even see that our mind is causing the interpretation. The meaning-making is causing the feelings.

The thought itself is causing the feeling. Keeping the event clearer, creating a distinction between what actually happened creates less pain. What "actually-factually" happened? "I invited them to dinner and they said 'no'."

Period.

If we don't put a period in there, then the mind will travel down a winding road.

Period. Period. Period...

There is less pain in stating the events factually. There's less feeling in the facts. There is less emotional upset, stress, suffering, worry, panic, terror.

"I invited her to dinner and she said no." What do our minds say happened? Our minds can go off on a fantasy adventure. "I can't trust her. I'm not important. She doesn't respect me." And our mind goes on *ad infinitum*, wrapping stories around what actually-factually happened.

Learning to clearly distinguish between facts and feelings has been very helpful for me personally. Growing up, my mother would yell. "She's yelling" is factual. But I would take it very personally. I would think, "She's yelling *at me*." And then a depth of feelings would rise up the second I felt she's yelling *at me* versus she's yelling. Period.

Without the period in there, my mind goes right off into she's yelling *at me*, and that *means* she doesn't care about me, I'm not safe around her, she's out of control, and all sorts of other thoughts that are much more terrifying than just witnessing and holding presence with a woman who happens to be yelling.

Radically, over time, I've even been able to understand where the yelling is coming from. To gain some compassion and humility about it. Even to reflect on the shape that *I'm* in when I find myself yelling.

Understand, discerning the difference between facts and feelings does not condone yelling. It doesn't make yelling good or bad or right or wrong. It just means we can be in the presence of someone yelling and be in the midst of the experience of someone yelling and actually-factually not take it personally. To understand their yelling belongs to them. It does not belong to you. And to the degree we can observe that and not absorb it, we're going to be in a higher mind, so to speak, or less regressed.

Let's apply this to something less threatening. What if someone doesn't call you back? Your feeling may be, "I'm so upset they didn't call me back."

What are the facts of the matter? They didn't return your call; they didn't call you back. Where would the emotion be in that if you were simply factual about it?

The mind loves to make up things. "They didn't call back." That's the facts of the matter. Which would be a passing thought, flowing into and out of our mind. *If* we weren't emotionally bound or emotionally reactive.

This passing thought would then lead to coherent thoughts, like, "Oh, I could call again. Perhaps they haven't gotten around to calling me back. Perhaps they didn't get my message."

Chapter 3

We would not make up a reason about why they've not called. We could just observe they haven't called back and stop right there.

The mind, instead of stopping right there, though, *loves* to make stuff up. "They didn't call me back! That means I'm not important, that means they don't care, that means they don't love me, that means they're going to ignore me. That means they think they're better than me, that means she's a witch." And so on.

If we don't catch our stampeding herd of thoughts, we will make up an entire story. We will then believe what we've made up. And we will begin to live in relationship to what we've just made up.

In reality, all that happened is: she didn't call back. Factual. Then our imagination operates, "She didn't call *me* back. It means I'm not important. She doesn't care. I can't trust her. She's not a good friend. I did something wrong," Blah, blah, blah, blah, blah. And then we believe what we've just made up. We've referenced and imagined all this past history, this past story, all the evidence to support our position to keep our already-drawn conclusions in place instead of coming from a place of knowing, "Oh, these are effects, these are feelings. This is made up, this is imagination!"

Our emotional bindings and our emotional reactivity are created in the imagination from our past, from our history, what we took on from our little formative years, times in our families of origin when we didn't get our way, and the meaning we made up around those incidents.

In this practice, we are creating and keeping a clear distinction between the feelings – the imagination and the emotional binds, the emotional reactivity – of making up something about what actually happened versus living from the facts of the matter.

"She didn't call back," leaves us empowered, resourceful, creative, innovative, thoughtful. And very focused on what it is we're wanting to achieve in leadership: clearer about our objectives and moving forward in their direction.

Chapter 4
Profess My Own Values and Beliefs Without Attacking or Judging

The key to mastering this skill is learning how to profess our own values and our own beliefs without expecting others to join us. Without *attacking* others for their beliefs, without even *judging* others for their beliefs. Sound impossible? It nearly is. It's a monumental accomplishment to actually profess our own beliefs and what we're convinced of, and not expect others to join us. To not expect you to do it my way, which is the "right way."

Your way is the wrong way, my way is the right way, right? So what's the problem?

The problem is the pain that we create for ourselves when we're in a judging, attacking, coaching, counseling, mentoring state of mind. It's painful when we try to do the impossible. It hurts when we try to get someone to change their beliefs, their own convictions. I can't even change *my* own convictions! It's delusional to think I can change another person's beliefs, versus them waking up to a change in their own way.

Let's look at this tool from a self-differentiation model, a measure of emotional and spiritual maturity, or effective leadership model. How can we profess our own beliefs and values and not judge another for theirs? How can we not drop and displace our expectations onto another, or to hold our expectations in a right and wrong frame. "I see it rightly, therefore you're wrong. My way's a good way, therefore yours is the bad or wrong way." As long as I'm framing situations in *that* way, there's always going to be *something* the matter with me.

There's always going to be the temptation to keep trying to do the impossible. To keep trying to change another person, or to change another person's beliefs, attitudes, judgments, dispositions, and patterns.

This would be no different from trying to teach a cat to bark, or trying to turn a human being into a giraffe, and then being frustrated as to why they are not changing.

You know what's *not* frustrating? Looking instead at the empowerment and the possibility of *me* being the one who actually changes.

I have friends in certain groups and arenas and causes that are very vegetarian, even veganism. They support the rights of animals, and are against abusing animals, exploiting them, or consuming animal products in any way. Over the years I've been challenged for eating meat.

I absolutely can appreciate and understand their desire for their cause. I support causes that lean toward veganism, are strictly vegan or vegetarian. I support animal-rescue sanctuaries and things like that. *And* I still consume meat. While it is not my value or my decision not to consume animal products, I absolutely can love and appreciate and understand it's somebody else's value and belief. And there's room for both. It doesn't have to be one or the other.

Another example of that is shaming. In my family, the elders shame the children. *Shame on you, shame on you.* I'm aware of how deep that shame is, not only in my own psyche, but in the psyche of human beings as a species. This deep, deep, deep well of shame exists in us.

Because of the meaning given to shaming, it makes my skin kind of crawl to hear anybody shaming another. Although it's not my way, I can absolutely understand the belief that shaming is a way to teach, a way to break habits, and to break patterns.

While it's not my belief, my value, or my way, it is certainly the way of some. My opposing others, or judging or attacking them for their way, only perpetuates more violence in the world.

In essence, if we see another as wrong, then we're shaming them for shaming, blaming them for blaming, judging them for judging or criticizing them for criticizing. When we fight against another person's belief—trying to eliminate these behaviors or minimize them in the world to create a world where these actions don't exist—we wind up perpetuating the very thing we claim we want to end or minimize in the world.

Chapter 5
Do Not Demand or Expect That Others Think, Feel, and Act Like You

Whenever I demand or expect that others should think, feel, and act like I do, I find myself thinking things like, "I never would have done it like that. What is she doing? I have done that for 100 years and I never would have done it the way she did. That is not a good way to do that. Has she been trained?"

How do we allow ourselves to have our way of doing things and not think, feel, demand, or expect that others are going to do it our way?

We're as unique as anything has been. Look at your little finger, and your little fingerprint. That's unique to you. With all the billions of us there are, each fingerprint is unique. And that's also how many unique ways we have of doing what we do.

When I believe any other person in the universe is going to do something the way I do it, the pain is on me, and the misery is on me, the suffering is on me. The suffering I have as a result of demanding, expecting, wanting, or even *should-ing* – that they *should* do it my way;

they *should* have considered me; they *should* follow my lead – is the source of my hell, my suffering, my misery, my tension, my stress. It's the source of the anxiety I'm experiencing.

Here's the good news. If I want less stress, less anxiety, less tension, I can drop expecting, demanding, or believing that any other person is going to do something the way I do it, or the way I think it ought to be done. This is how we take back the power we have.

When we demand, expect, and displace power onto somebody else, we give away all our power in the situation. We take back that power when we say, "I do it the way I do it. That makes sense to me. They do it the way they do it, because that makes sense to them. It reflects the consciousness they're in. It reflects the belief and the thought they're having at the time."

This isn't mysterious. Just like you and me, each person has his or her own way of doing things. When we dismantle the "right and wrong" frame, and the "good and bad" frame, we have less emotional reactivity to whatever others do—and even *how* they do it.

Taking back your power leaves you more responsive and less reactive. It leaves you more thoughtful, and puts you in the mindset of being a student. You begin to ask yourself, "Can I learn from them, as well?" It requires an open mind to be willing to learn anything, a willingness to accept differences between people, as we'll see in the next chapter.

Chapter 6
Accept Differences Between People

In the circles I run in and in the classes I present (for organizations, companies, businesses, neighborhoods, families, and ministries) people in the room often state, "We are like-minded. We think alike." It's not true. Sometimes we think alike, sometimes we do not. This unwillingness and this denial to accept and acknowledge that we actually have differences is delusional.

It's delusional and problematic because when our natural differences arise, we become opposed to them or affronted by them or afraid of them. We begin judging, attacking, and demanding we all be the same. Until we accept differences in ourselves, in people closest to us, those we work with, live with, associate with, attend church with, people living in the same community as us, or doing our same jobs, we judge and attack. Until we learn to accept our differences, we are subject to and hostage to those differences.

Let me give you a personal example: I *love* crab legs. I

love them so much I often used to say that if I ever knew it was my last meal, I would want it to be crab legs.

The family I was raised in feels differently. Not only do they not want a crab leg, and would not eat a crab leg, they don't even want to be at a table with me while I'm eating crab legs because the smell is so offensive to them.

So where does that leave me if I'm eating with my family, and they feel so strongly about crab legs, and I want to eat crab legs? It's up to me to accept the difference in us and then measure if I'm going to push or force or demand my way. Do I want crab legs no matter what their reaction will be?

Or do I want to lean more toward not eroding the relationship and not ruining the time we have together for a meal? Accepting these differences, I'm going to eat crab legs with *other* people, not with my family. Making this choice is not to give in or not honoring myself. It's simply to say, in this case, "I want to give intentional time and care to my relationships." I want that healthy relationship more than I want to eat crab legs even if it's offending somebody.

The same can be true where there are allergies. One of my friends is allergic to peanuts and it took me years to understand just how much fear is around that allergy; to understand what can happen with allergies to food where breathing is absolutely shut down or obstructed in some way.

It was not a funny matter for me to say "It's not that big of a deal" to have peanuts in the house or peanuts in the car when they're with me because I wanted peanuts and I wanted them *now*. It's hard for me to scientifically understand how someone can have a reaction if they're not eating the peanuts, that if they're in the same space, they're still under some type of allergic effect. Even though I don't fully understand the fear or the allergic reaction, I choose the relationship, the friendship, over peanuts when I am with this person.

It's also about accepting differences between people's styles. Some people wake up all Chatty Cathy in the morning and others need space and time and quiet and are not interested in launching into a conversation.

Over the years, I've learned to adapt to other people's styles and not force my way. To allow them the space they need to have their coffee, or have their silence so they can come out into the world in their own time, on their own schedule, on their own routine.

Get a sense of what the consequences are to you when you find yourself not accepting that there are differences between you and others. What does it create in your household or workplace when you think people should be the same, should think the same, eat the same, show up the same way, even worship the same way or have the same philosophies about employment or jobs or politics? What are the consequences to you of not accepting that we have differences? What does denying differences cause in your own life?

What would it be like to accept that we do have differences so it's not a problem when we encounter differences? Then there would be nothing to be afraid of, nothing to make us reactive.

What would it be like to accept differences with the people closest to you, the people you work with, the places you shop? What would it be like to know that just because we have differences, it doesn't mean that we really differ?

What would it be like to realize that we represent the full spectrum of being human, and that within this spectrum, whatever's happening through me, as me, through them, as them, is *always* within the human phenomenon?

Whatever they're thinking, whatever they're doing, is a representation of part of our own humanity. We can accept the fullness of that humanity; the wholeness of experiencing both beliefs, not "one or the other." Or we can continue to be victim to—and hostage to—our wanting something to be one way while denying and fearing it being another way.

Accepting differences in other people absolutely requires me to grow myself up and allow the full spectrum of human beings to *be* human beings and to quickly and powerfully awaken to our differences in all cases.

Over time, regardless how similar we are, or how close we are, or if we were raised in the same house, or are in the same family, or in the same profession—there are *absolutely* differences between each of us and every other person on the planet. And that's nothing to be upset about.

Chapter 7
Take Responsibility for Your Own Anger

Taking responsibility for our own anger can be a bitter pill to swallow. It's hard to think about this idea. And it's certainly not all that popular when I offer it in workshops and seminars. Even suggesting the notion that it's time to grow ourselves up, that we're going to have to take responsibility for our own anger, creates a gut reaction, a push-back. Especially as we realize it's not just our *anger* we're responsible for. We're also responsible for our sadness, despair, frustrations, stress, or any discomfort whatsoever.

"Me? How can I be responsible for my own anger when she's the matter with me?"

As leaders, regardless of what another person is doing, the question is, *how am I going to respond to this?* Regardless of what they're doing—whatever they're saying, accusing, blaming me of, criticizing me for—none of it is mine.

I cannot change someone else's aspect. What I can change is how I respond to the situation. Our job is to learn how not to blame anybody else for the feelings we are having.

Whoa! This changes everything! Personal responsibility is counterintuitive. Since we've been three, four, even five years old, we have blamed whoever was in our field for our sadness, despair, upset; for our being afraid. We looked to them, and made them responsible for the shape we were in. We expected our parents to protect us, to provide for us, to take responsibility for our feelings. To soothe us when we had upset feelings. And that four-year-old in us is still running the show.

Our maturity depends on us taking responsibility for our own emotions. No longer blaming anybody else for our stress, our upset, sadness, or anything else. What stops you from taking responsibility for your own emotions? What are the consequences to you if you continue to blame somebody else for your emotions?

Taking responsibility for our anger puts us back in our own power. It also keeps us from scapegoating anybody else or displacing the pain, discomfort, and anger through blaming—which is the mind's knee-jerk reaction.

Taking responsibility for our own discomfort invites, allows, and encourages us to make room for our feelings. To accept that human suffering is a natural part of our life processes, that it's absolutely part of anger, pain, sadness, and despair.

Every emotion is part of our learning and growing process. We don't have to live as victim to those emotions, or in any other immature relationship with these emotions.

From a leader's perspective, ponder for yourself what are the consequences to your leadership quality, and your leadership capabilities, if you dump your responsibility on somebody else? How is that going to inhibit you from leading?

When we take responsibility for our own discomfort, how would we be better leaders? What would we model for others? What would I teach others if I were to say, *"Oh, wow. I'm responsible for my own discomfort?"*

Naturally we're going to expect and believe that others can do the same for themselves when we do this for ourselves. We model for others how to assume responsibilities for their own emotions, their own discomfort. We model for others how they, too, can restore themselves—as we're able to for ourselves—so they can then model this awareness for others.

Be aware of the mind that would want to resist the opportunity to take responsibility for our own anger.

This mind is the one that says, *"Wait a minute. I'm not taking responsibility for my own emotions. I'm going to continue to blame others. This is nonsense. You don't live with my mother. This is nonsense. You've never been criticized by my boss like I'm criticized by my boss."*

Regardless of the situation, regardless of the person, regardless of the criticism, think about the disempowerment you experience when you hold someone else responsible for your emotions. Then realize the empowerment that's possible when you begin to take responsibility for your own emotional state.

Disempowerment, empowerment. If there's a point of choice, that point is the only place in the universe where we have any control.

This is the place where we have a real capacity to

respond instead of react, to be more thoughtful and less knee-jerked, less instinctual, less automatic in our response. We become able to actually make a choice that is more coherent, more effective, and more affective as leaders, parents, spouses, siblings, and human beings.

Tea Break

Congratulations for investing in yourself for the sake of others in your life. This is a selfless sacrifice for the benefit of others while also fulfilling and growing yourself. Here are some words to keep you motivated:

"Make sane sensible choices that move you in the direction of your own goals."

"When you notice the horse is dead - dismount. Whatever you are "riding" is dead. Dismount."

"Choose your actions based on what makes your "tail" wag."

Chapter 8
Live by Your Own Goals

Living by our own goals means living by what interests us and not by the goals and expectations other people have for us. Living by my own goals has been one of the most challenging tenets of Presence and Potential. I had been so patterned and programmed into pleasing others and going along with others to keep the peace—peace at any price— that I literally didn't know what the goals for my own life were in some cases.

I was the oldest of three children in my family, born to parents who were both the youngest in their family. I was dedicated to keeping things going; doing whatever we had to do to keep things moving along. Including keeping the peace.

Back then, my ways of trying to keep peace were not very effective—especially when my goals came up against conflicting goals within my family. I would often set aside my goals for the goals of another, the goals of the family, the goals of keeping peace.

Chapter 8

It's miraculous how well I've been able to continuously and consistently move in the direction of my goals, despite my habit of relegating my goals to the back seat.

For example, my family didn't go to church, and I wanted to go to church. When I told my mother, she told me, "Go find your way to go to church; find someone to take you."

So I did. I called the neighbors and they took me to church, which I loved very much. I loved going. I loved my Sunday school teacher and memorizing scripture and things like that. Even though it wasn't part of my family tradition, it was important to me, so I took action to move in the direction of my own goals.

I also loved playing softball and I was popular playing softball. I was a good athlete. I played softball five nights a week on five different teams. I had very specific chores at home that had to be done in order for me to go play in the evenings. So, I worked hard to keep laundry done and the housework and chores and cleaning done and schoolwork and everything else—so I could meet my goal to play all the softball I had the opportunity to play.

As I got older, I had sincere desires to travel. When I first moved to Nashville, in 1989, I worked at a large corporation. I wanted to travel and didn't have the extra money. I had just taken on a mortgage and was paying for college and other things that were important to me. Yet I wanted to travel.

An opportunity came up to work for American Airlines out on the ramp, helping park airplanes, loading bags and things like that. Back then, any employee of American Airlines travelled free as long as there was space available. I worked 9-5 in my corporate job and drove out to the airport and worked there from 6-10 at night, just so I could travel for free.

I've done many, many things to move myself in the direction of my goals for my life. I've also had a lot of challenge and pushback and questioning and discouragement at times, for the paths I was taking—because they often didn't make sense. My goals often looked like they were too hard, or undoable or that I was too dreamy to meet some of them.

Today, I'm very grateful that I've been able to exercise this commitment to myself and—in most cases—constantly, consistently and persistently move in the direction of my own goals.

So, when I say, "Live by your own goals," it often begs the question. How do you even know what your personal goals are? What interests you? Who do you want to be in this or any interaction? Not how do you *usually* do it, not how do *they* do it—but how do you want to be in your life?

What is a life that's interesting to you? What are you going to look back from on your death bed and say, "Wow, that's exactly what I wanted to do!" "Wow, I thought for myself!" "Wow, I didn't let their upset, their threats, their needs, their wants, and their 'shoulds' impact me so much that I wasn't able to make a choice based on what was integral, honest action for me."

Start small. Find an area in your life where you feel you're living out somebody else's expectations for you. Where you didn't have enough self to say, "You know, no, I'm not going to do that." Or "That doesn't interest me. That doesn't make sense to me." Or even, "That's against my own integrity to do that." The emotional binds we're in have caused us to do these things instead of what was truly ours to do. Imagine what it would be like to say, "I really get that you want this for me. I really understand why —*and* it's simply not honest action for me." Or "It's not a goal I have for my own life."

Such defining moments in my life have occurred when I've been able to live by my own goals. In the few little places I've been able to say, "I get that you want this for me. I get why you want this for me. That you naturally want for me something that's benefited you or that's changed your life. I get that that's why you would want me to do it. And it's just an absolute simple and honest no for me. That is not a goal that I have for my own life."

It certainly is of interest for me to continue to do that self-honoring, including specific ways of even how I'm a facilitator.

Some of the college and ordination education I have is very non-traditional. I went to night school, day school, took early college classes, correspondence courses. I got all the credits I could for college without ever living on a college campus. Other people wanted me to live on a college campus. They wanted me to have that experience. And I saw another way to do it that seemed more honest for me at the time. So even with the pressures to do it the way "everybody else" does it, I was able to define myself and say, "There's another way for me here."

I found colleges that provided accelerated learning that really caused me to step up and make decisions to work full-time and go to school-full time. That would not have been suitable at all for others. That could have been enough to cause a system breakdown, or to cause them to throw in the towel on all of it. But it worked well for me. Even though it could have finished somebody else off, it was directly in alignment with my own energy and my capabilities.

The invitation here is to self-examine. "Am I doing something under pressure of others, to be liked, to be okay, to be accepted, to be understood? Or am I living in accordance with the goals of my own life?"

Find ways of how you're *not* doing this. It's not a question of are you doing this? "Yes. There are things I'm doing that I don't really care a lick about. There are things I'm doing that I'm doing under pressure because it's always been done this way, or because someone else has expectations of me to do it that way."

When we awaken to those, determine where those are, then it's possible for us to say, "I can come back then to what is more interesting to me. What is more in alignment with the goals I have for my life? How do I define my own life? How do I live according to my own goals, with the pressures and the expectation of others still in place? How can I not try to manage the expectations of others, but instead make choices that are more in integrity with the goals for my own life?"

Chapter 9
Refuse to Coerce, Will, and Threaten Other People Into Going Along With You

In addition to refusing to coerce, will, and threaten other people into going along with you, I would add a few more refusals. Refuse to charm, seduce, manipulate, and control others into going along with you. Great anxiety is caused by the effort of trying to coerce somebody else to go along with us. To have others believe the way we do, to think the way we do, to understand where we're coming from.

Practicing this principle has been a little easier for me than some other principles. I'm more prone to say things like *it's fine, it's fine. It doesn't matter, it's okay, anything is fine with me. Whatever.*

I'm more likely to go along with the group or go along with the majority. Or simply stay quiet. I'm not as prone to coercing, willing, or threatening other people to go along with my way.

However, I am absolutely known as a master at *influencing* people to go along with my way, by encouraging and inspiring. By using enthusiasm and excitement to get their buy-in. I understand that—depending on the energy around my efforts and what is motivating me to do it—this influencing can also be coercion.

Even enthusiasm or inspiration can be manipulative at times, and controlling at times. Particularly if it's being done with somebody who is showing resistance or who has clearly stated their lack of interest in something.

It's important to continuously look not just at *if* we coerce, but *how* we coerce. Although we may not threaten other people, we may still use other subtle and not so subtle approaches of influence to get people to go along with our ideas or our way of doing things, our timeline or our way of thinking or being. It's a form of recruitment. And the energy to do that is not sustainable over time.

I find it's also not in integrity for me to do that. It's very important to me to catch these tendencies in myself and to back up and to clean that up, so to speak, before I proceed. Because I don't want to be influenced, willed, threatened, manipulated, controlled, seduced, and charmed by other people either.

Even just writing that is an energy drain on me. The fullness of energy that was present when I began to think about coercing, getting others to think my way, began to drain away. An immense expense of time and energy and effort goes out trying to change the impossible, trying to change what somebody else is doing, thinking, or believing.

How would everyone be better off if we stopped that? For example, I once took it on as my responsibility to get my little nephew—whom I love more than anything in the world—to brush his teeth. I built a chart for him to track how he brushed his teeth, and how often. I gave him rewards and incentives for brushing his teeth.

Then one day I awakened to how much that is not mine to do. My fear was draining me. My underlying fear was that he actually would lose his teeth; that he actually would not have teeth if he didn't take care of his teeth in a regimental way. That truth was not all that uncommon in our family. My parents and other elders lost their teeth as early as age 40. They either didn't have dentures, never got dentures, or had all their teeth pulled or something like that.

As a result of my familial experiences, I had a fear of this same fate for this child. One day I woke up to the truth that "This is not mine to do—he's perfectly capable of doing this for himself." And I just stopped it. I was able to just stop it. I get big laughs out of this today because he has this great big smile and these beautiful, beautiful teeth. Somehow, he knew to brush. How to, and when to didn't require Aunt Martha's intervention on that. It's just one little example of how I've used my own coercion and taken on somebody else's responsibility to be my own.

Our patterns in this area—and our unawareness of our patterns— has us bound up. How do we wake up to our actions? Where am I doing each of these methods? And with whom? What's causing us to make these choices? What it would be like to simply stop this behavior? To stop trying to coerce, will, threaten, seduce, manipulate, and control other people to be different than they are?

In organizations and in our family; in relationships, with children, with everyone we meet? How would we be better off to stop that behavior?

Chapter 10

Refuse to Be Coerced, Willed and Threatened by Other People

After we begin to refuse to coerce, will, threaten, or become stubborn, charming, or use other methods trying to get somebody else to change, our next step is to refuse to be willed, coerced and threatened by others.

The most poignant memory I have using this tenet is with the person I love the most in the world, my baby brother Randy. He was my closest relationship. He was born when I was eight, so I was very motherly with him. He always had me—and most of the family—wrapped around his little finger with how loveable and charming he was.

On a cold December night many, many years ago, our dad was in his last months of living and I had gone home to care for him.

I notified Randy that if he came to daddy's house drinking—which he was prone to do—I would not let him in. I told him he was welcome there, and I hoped he would come and be a part of our dad's life. *And* he would not be able to do that if he came there drinking; I would not let him in the house.

I'm sure he didn't believe anything I said about that. I had tried to set boundaries and limits with him for decades and had not done so very well. So, it was no surprise he didn't take it any more seriously than he would have a butterfly fluttering by.

He came by late one cold dark December night, and he was drunk. I told him he couldn't come in the house. He began his flow chart with me of behaviors that started with charm, giggling, charisma, *lighten up* he would say, *you need a drink sis, that's what you need. You need to take yourself a drink. I'm not that drunk*, justifying, explaining.

He tried everything that had always worked with me.

On that particular night, though, I was able to say to him, *you can't come in, honey. I'm going to say no to this.*

He responded by moving into guilting, shaming, *you think you run the world, you think you're the boss of everything, you think you run the show, everything's got to be your way, you're not the boss of me. This is not your house. He's my father, too.* Everything under the sun he could think of, he said to me, to get me to fold.

Any one of these tactics would have worked in the past. On that particular night, none of them had any real effect on me. He saw his efforts were not working, and he moved on to what he was confident *would* work: threatening to kill himself.

I don't have any place to go. It's 12 degrees outside. If I can't come in here, I'll freeze to death in the car. When you wake up tomorrow, I'm gonna be dead. You want me to be dead. Your life would be better off if I was dead. I know how this works; you would be so better off if you didn't have the likes of me bothering you.

I held my ground. *I know I don't want you dead. For sure, I don't want you to freeze to death . . . and you can't come in.*

Eventually he had run the gamut of everything from the past that would have coerced me — guilt, willfulness, stubbornness, threats to self, threats to me — everything that had worked in the past, for forty-some years.

That night none of it had the same effect on me. It was the first time in our relationship together. That particular night, I was able to define myself with him, and not cut off from him. I was able to love him and care about him *and* look him in the eye and simply say "You're right, you're right *and* you can't come in."

He left. He didn't freeze to death. He went right on down the road like he always did. I've often said my brother was more resourceful drunk than the smartest people I know are sober. And I got to see an example of his skills that night.

With practice, you can keep a clear distinction between what is *theirs* and what is *yours*. You can keep a clear distinction between why another person is coming from the place they are. You can have more understanding about that, *and* still absolutely refuse to be willed, coerced, or threatened into doing something, just because they want it, just because they believe you should, just because they think you need to. You absolutely can declare, "No, I'm going to think for myself." From this space, you can take action based on what is true for you, what is in integrity for you. You'll be less enmeshed in the emotional binds of somebody else, trying to appease them, go along with them, keep peace, be liked, or be understood. Refuse to do it to others, and refuse for others to do it to you. Take back your own responsibility and your own power for what you can and cannot do, what you will and won't do, and to live and stand in your own conviction of that.

Chapter 11
Keep Relationships Open

Keeping our relationships with other people open starts with avoiding gossiping. That'll finish a few of us off, if we actually stopped gossiping. Just think about what it would do for our lives to stop gossiping.

Stopping gossip may seem counter-intuitive, because we have taught people to gossip with us. We say, "Come, let's talk about John. Let's rake John over the coals. Let's make John our enemy." We put so much focus on John— whomever your John is—and what he's doing, that we seldom ever pause to look to see, "What am I thinking? What's going on with me? What can I actually do something about here?"

Shifting our focus from the external, which is *them* and what *they're* doing, we can shift back to the internal. "What am I doing? How am I in relationship to this? How am I in response to this? What can we talk about besides somebody else? How can I teach this new way I'm going to relate to you by only talking about each other, and not somebody else?"

For me, making this shift means I keep my relationship with you open. It means I avoid what is secretive, I avoid what is collusive, I avoid what is gossipy, and what is not mine to be talking about in the first place., Then, if somebody presents to me and says, "Hey, let's talk about John," I might respond, "I'm really working on not talking about people who aren't here. Instead of talking about John, let's talk about us. Let's talk about you and me. Let's talk about something we can do *something* about."

This has been very powerful for my life. It still is hard work. I'm not immune from getting caught up in relationship-closing gossip, believe me. Keeping relationships open is hard work. It's also extremely important and powerful work. It ensures our relationship with another person is not going to be actually with and about that other person; not about a third person.

For example, if I'm talking with my mother, I want to talk about my mother and myself. I want to keep my relationship with my mother open and not make the focus of my relationship to my mother about what my brother's doing, what my nephew's doing or what the neighbor's doing.

Instead, I focus only on my mother and myself. "What's going on in you? What's happening with your life? What's happening in mine?"

This practice allows us to relate on a one-to-one open relationship, internally-focused, present to who's in front of us and less externally focused on whomever can be the displacement for our judgments, our wants and needs, and shoulds and should nots. We begin forming open one-to-one relationships, avoiding secrets—which is collusive—

and we bring whatever is externally focused into focus on the current moment.

Relationships are central to my way of being. They're essential to my life. I put the highest priority on relationships. I have as high a priority on relationships in my life as any other thing in my life. Professionally, personally, family, and otherwise.

Keeping relationships open includes speaking directly to somebody, going directly to the source. This is one of the most important practices I've had throughout my life. I work at it all the time, even when it's hard, difficult, and uncomfortable.

If I find I have a hard feeling, it's important to me to be authentic about that in my conversations. It's the difference between speaking *with* someone versus speaking *to* someone or *about* someone. It's the opposite of gossiping, venting, blaming, and shaming.

What does this look like for me? I'll go to someone directly and say, *I felt bad about this*, or, *My feelings were hurt about this*, or, *I wanted to talk about this*, or, *I feel like there's something going on in our relationship that I want to reconcile or resolve.*

Direct, one-on-one communication with folks is the core of true open relationships, emotionally. To chat directly *with* someone instead of *about* them. To have the scary conversations instead of sticking my head in the sand, avoiding or pretending something's not going on. Those avoidance techniques have not been effective. I'm very proud of the way I'm able to do this and I'm also understanding of myself at times when I can't do it.

When are we less likely to have direct conversations? When we don't have the energy or stamina for them.

When we don't feel the conversation will be effective. When we're afraid of how the other person will respond or react. When we fear they'll be volatile or hyper-angry or out of control. That's when we're not as likely to keep our relationships open; at least it's when I'm not as likely to do it.

Even though it takes a demonstrated amount of persistence and courage to continue this practice, you may find yourself highly committed to doing the practice, based on how much relationships—with yourself, with peace and with others—mean to you.

Chapter 12
Change My Position from Victimization to What Can I Do

One of my most basic life tenets is to look at what *can* be done in a situation and to ask myself what would be a sane and sensible action in that situation. Regardless of what has happened, regardless of what went down, regardless of the pain, the situation or circumstances, regardless of anything, my question is always the same: *what can I do here?*

This practice may be one of my very favorite ones. Shifting my position, my belief systems, my thought systems, from *"I'm a victim, I'm a victim here, I've been victimized here!"* to "What can I do?"

Asking this question is the greatest empowerment. It's the opposite of crying over spilled milk or becoming resigned to what's done or what can't be changed or undone. Regardless of what happened or who's hurt or what the circumstances are, it's empowering to back up and look at what can be done, from this point forward.

Bringing a situation into the present creates a sense of grace; gives you room to speak about what you *can* do versus *coulda, woulda, shoulda.*

This tool was very valuable to me in 2008 when I was diagnosed with breast cancer. As I received the actual-factual reporting of breast cancer and what the approach to this breast cancer could be, it was very important to me not to feel victimized about this diagnosis and to keep a broad perspective instead. I looked at all the medical conditions and medical circumstances and losses that other people have in their lives with diseases ranging from A to Z. From this vantage point my breast cancer diagnosis— compared to the entire human spectrum of diseases— seemed extremely minor to me.

It was important to me to approach this diagnosis with an attitude of *this is what is.* And from there, I could ask myself, *what can I do with what is? What is the sane and sensible action to do here?*

By not choosing to be a victim to *what is*, I became more of a victor. I was empowered to get through whatever treatments and surgeries and procedures required, with an absolute depth of gratitude. I didn't like it, certainly didn't love it, and definitely wouldn't want to have cancer or do the treatments again. And, in the big scheme of things, I found peace within the perspective: *what's a little breast cancer?*

So too, in any situations in life, you have the power to ask yourself, *what can I do?* "In this relationship, what can I do? In this circumstance, what can I do?" There's a big difference between, a victimized, despaired, "Oh, no - I've lost my job, what am I going to do!" or an empowered "I've lost my job. What am I going to do?" That difference changes your entire reality. That changes your absolute experience of life. This is vastly different from victim-thinking where "something's being done to me," and we are therefore at the mercy of—and a victim to—everything, including the traffic jam, the rainy day, the burnt toast, or an undercooked egg. This is empowering thinking.

With this practice, we embrace life on life's terms. Life is doing what life does. How we relate to life is up to us. Now we can relate to life on life's terms. We can ask, "What can I do in this situation, what can I do in this interaction?" Herein lies all the power of the universe. Making the shift from being a victim to a can-doer. What can you do here?

Chapter 13
Gain Space and Time and a Broader Perspective About Anything

The way we see the world is very limited. It's a little limited scope of what we each are seeing. It's a mindset that tells us *this is what's happening here. This is what* always *happens.*

In this practice, we explore how to gain space to say, "Well, no, now hold on. What if I could see that incident just a little more clearly? What if I could get an even broader perspective here? Let me check with somebody else on how they would see this. What's their experience here?"

Instead of coming at everything with the same old, instinctual, automatic pattern, what would it do for me to pause and say, "Let me take some time and space. Let me get a higher view of this."

A song about seeing things from higher ground comes to mind. What would it do for me to take a higher ground, to get a broader perspective, to unglue and unstick and unbind ourselves from seeing a situation from the extremely limited, little narrow way we've always seen it?

If our minds were open and fluid enough, we would have the ability to step back and look at a broader perspective. We could consider where other people are coming from, relate to what may have caused them to do something, understand their thinking patterns and beliefs —the shape they're in, so to speak.

This practice has brought a great deal of understanding to me. Regardless of circumstances, I'm committed to relating to what others may be thinking and doing, which gives me a broader perspective.

Stepping back for a broader perspective has also kept me from being as instinctive and reactive as I would have been otherwise. When I don't stop to think and put a pause in my response, and don't consider the bigger picture, I'm more apt to be knee-jerkish, slipping into my own, outdated, painful patterns of being.

By keeping a broader perspective when listening to my family, I have, over time, been able to see the influence they had from *their* parents and *their* grandparents that highly influenced the ways they are in the world. Doing family-of-origin work, looking at the generations above my parents, and the generations above that, gave me a lot of insight into how my expanded family was being in the world.

I can look at the two extremes of my family's patterns around work for example. At one end, people were working extremely hard, day-in and day-out, being workaholic types —which is more the way I leaned in. I was working seven days a week and looking for things to do even when I may have a day off, or even a free hour.

At the other extreme is where we found family members who were committed to not do much at all. Not having a job, being unemployed, and going days, years, and weeks without working. Not thinking about what's coming, about how the year-end bills will get paid, and so on. My family is full of tales about not planning. One story has it that winter arrived and they ran out of wood, and somebody was shocked that there was no wood, as if they hadn't even noticed they were running out of wood. That work style has carried on in some parts of our family today.

I was "shocked" at how unprepared one person may be for something that seemed so predictable to me. Keeping a broader perspective that this cycle is generations deep in my family has brought me an understanding toward our differences. Whether it is the sins of the father passed down, or whether it's just the way we're wired, or the mystery of life, I accept it.

Practice keeping a broader perspective about the way people are, the way they behave, the way they react, the way they work or don't work, the way they value education, or how they clean their house or dress or whatever else.

This principle has been very freeing, more and more. It's a practice to have less reactivity and less concern about others' ways; less meddling in somebody else's business. We put forth less judgment on somebody else whenever we step back and gain a new view, focusing on leaning toward holding a broader perspective about anything we perceive.

Think about this from a leadership perspective. What are the consequences of not taking space and time and keeping a broader perspective? What are the consequences when we continue to do things the way we've always done them? What are some of the consequences to a ministry, to an organization, or to a relationship, when we don't put this into practice?

Chapter 13

Over time, most relationships and organizations couldn't survive in that environment. Not only would they decline, they might actually die—because we're built to grow, expand, change and evolve. We're compelled and often rewarded by a universal force to be different, to expand. And if we do not allow our own mind to have that kind of expansiveness, to take a broader perspective, then we're blind to all the possible ways to do something beyond the ways we've always done it.

Presence Break

You're halfway through the book and closer to your goals than ever before.

"We teach people how to treat us. If we act like a doormat then we are going to get stepped on."

"I don't have to love what is ... I don't even have to like it, but I don't have to be at "war"with it either."

"Do I want to be "right", or do I want to have "peace?""

Whispers of Wisdom (card deck)

Need more wisdom like this on hand and in hand? Try the *Whispers of Wisdom cards*, available on Martha's site at

https://uppa-creek-art.myshopify.com/products/whispers-of-wisdom-inspirational-card-deck

Chapter 14
Contain Your Own Reactivity When Others Are Reacting

Remember the herd effect? What are the consequences to me in my own life if I get just as reactive as they do? Then there's no one thinking here. There's no one resourceful. It's as if I'm concealing that, "They're a goner, and I'm a goner with them to the degree that I react—even in the slightest —to their reactions toward me.

Imagine what it would feel and look like to contain your own reactivity when others are reacting. The more jacked-up another person gets, the calmer you get. The more confrontational and loud the other is, the more you're able to understand, the more you're able to listen. The more threatening and volatile they may become, the more coherent and aware of your options you become. The more clearly you think, the less reactive you are in response to their reactivity.

This is one of the top practices people ask about when I present these teachings. What does it actually mean to contain my own reactivity? So many examples will be familiar to you. Here are two common examples of this principle in practice:

When somebody else is yelling, don't yell. When somebody else is getting angrier and angrier, regulate yourself so you don't get as jacked-up and amped-up and anxious as they are.

If I get as reactive as another person, now there are two of us being reactive. And the more reactive I become, the less listening I can do, the lower my functioning goes, and the more things escalate.

Containing my own reactivity is not just good for me and my well-being, but for the well-being of the relationship and the well-being of the whole of humanity. All it takes is for one of us, the strongest among us, to be able to take a deep breath and soften up. If somebody else can't soften—if they're getting more rigid—we can choose to get more flexible, instead of joining them or pushing back or resisting.

Even when someone's getting sadder and sadder, it's not helpful for me to join them in their pain or in their misery. It's not going to ease the situation for me to commiserate with them versus being able to witness their misery and to hold a more neutral stance while understanding the normality of their reaction as a human learning processes. Even in that knowing, I can absolutely hold a space of equanimity and not get as reactive as they are, whether the reaction they're having is angry, sad, mad, righteous, indignant, violent, rageful, or whatever.

There is real benefit to any relationship, if one person can hold a less anxious presence in the face of somebody else's reactivity.

Contain Your Own Reactivity When Others Are Reacting

Looking at your own life, how can you contain your reactivity regardless of what another is doing? How can you contain your reactivity, especially when they can't? How can you contain your reactivity regardless of how upset, loud, confrontational, accusing, they are? How can you be in this situation, in this circumstance, more calm and less reactive?

As a leader of whatever you're leading—your family, your organization, your neighborhood—the power that you have when you are able to do this practice within your leadership system has absolute value. The effects on a system are powerful whenever just one of us can be a little less reactive—even when other people are being reactive.

Chapter 15
Take a Stand and Be Less Anxious

Imagine there's a vote going around where you have to give a *yes* or *no* answer. Whatever way you decide, you're going to state your vote and then offer up your thinking about your vote. "Here's my thinking. Here's what I think about this, here's what I think we ought to do. So this is what I'm thinking. This is my belief about this. This is my concern if we go this way. This is what I believe could happen if we go that way." When we're not anxious about how we're going to vote or why we would vote a particular way, we take a stand.

With less attachment comes less anxiety, we become less concerned about anyone else voting one way or another. We become less interested in having others agree or support our position.

Now imagine someone asks you for money, for a loan, for an advance. How anxious are you about how your answer will be perceived?

People have asked to borrow money from me more times than I can count throughout my life. I've looked at this experience many, many times to see what makes me the target for asking, and how people seem so comfortable in asking.

In my early life, as a young girl and even through my twenties, thirties and forties, I was like a community banker. My practice was to be a revolving door, handing out money whenever people wanted to borrow the money.

Over time people were not actually *borrowing* money; I was *giving* them money. Giving money is never a loan until the day it is paid back. That's what makes it a loan. Until the money was paid back, I was giving—not lending—money.

Having that new perspective shifted things for me. It also helped me to be less anxious about what I give. I realized it was not on them, it was on me. If I'm going to give money, I acknowledged my responsibility to not call it a loan until it was paid back. Before that awareness, calling it a loan made it stressful, and made me more anxious about the money given.

In my early life this stress led me to track payments, and call the people who had received the money, and ask for payment plans, and promissory notes to be signed. It led to promises made and promises broken. Plans made and plans broken. Then, over time, the stress led to just actually giving it up.

I took a stand. I forgave all the debts that anybody had to me and for me, which was a great big step in freeing myself and taking that anxiety away. I accepted that how I had been giving was based on naive misunderstandings and patterned behavior on my part.

As I became less judgmental of myself, I took myself off the hook. And I took them off the hook. Over the last few years, I've found myself able to be more discerning; more able to say *yes* when it's an actual *yes*, and *no* when it's an actual *no*. And I'm not as afraid to say *no*, regardless of who's asking, or under what circumstances.

I'm hoping and praying that I have had my last rodeo with this *and* I know the people closest to me are where I still have the biggest difficulty. I want to share, big-hearted; I want to hand out and give away and make dreams come true and make bucket lists come true.

Over-functioning, becoming over-responsible, is a tender tightrope that teeters very close to taking responsibility for other people. In some situations, the more responsible and over-functioning *we* get, the less and less responsible *they* get. By our actions, others become more prone to under-functioning. To break this cycle, it's incumbent on us to be able to take a stand, and tell the truth about what's motivating us to give or not give, and to give more and more honest *yes's*, and more and more honest *no's*.

Take a stand. Take a stance. Offer why. Outline your thinking. As you do, you'll send forth a less anxious presence, less anxiety, less tension. More willingness for others to have their own thinking process. And less attachment to others having to go along with your way of thinking.

Chapter 16
Do Not Confuse Closeness and Sameness

Just because I'm close to you doesn't mean we're the same. Dr. Murray Bowen, pioneer of family systems therapy, speaks about the internal forces of togetherness and separation. There is no denying both are inherent in us. We have an innate desire to be close to people, to be intimate, and with others. We also have a desire to be independent, to be individual, to be separate from.

But not too separate. When we get too separate, we get uncomfortable. We're pulled back to being close again. Then we get too close and then we are driven to find some separation again. This pull is always going on, like a pendulum, back and forth.

In the arenas where I work and play and operate relationship-wise—professionally and personally—I often hear that we are *likeminded*. We have a desire or belief to feel close to people when we feel we're the same; we begin to believe we can relate better to likeminded people, or that we're cut from the same cloth.

This tendency to feel close is problematic because we're always going to have times of closeness and times of separation, times of closeness and intimacy and times of distancing and living more separate lives.

This internal force that we have about closeness is always moving in us. The minute we get too close and too intimate with somebody, we'll have discomfort about that. Notice when you have that discomfort. And notice when you feel others are starting to be too close, too clingy, too needy, too demanding, saying things like, "I miss you. I've got to hear from you. Where are you? When are we going to be together? I've not had enough time with you."

You know this from your relationships. There are times when we just can't get close enough to another. And then, there are times when we need space. When we feel smothered, even.

That's an example of this closeness, believing that if we're close we're the same versus we are not the same. And that there's an internal pressure in us, built into us, instinctual in us, to be close while also being a separate individual. To know where I begin and end, to know where you begin and end, and then discovering how we can be in relationship without taking over one another, and without being separated out of anxiety and pulled together by anxiety. But rather understanding the flow of it. At times our connection will be close, and at times it's going to be separate.

When I'm not uncomfortable and freaked out and worried when our connection is in a particular state, I can understand that the current state will change, just like the wind. This knowledge brings some comfort, and then more comfort. This practice teaches how to tolerate the current position and how to build tolerance and acceptance of this position so it's not a good or bad place. We can then look at each state of closeness and sameness and determine, "This is not good. This is not bad. This is both—and part of the human phenomena."

How can you increase your acceptance and toleration to the position in which you find yourself, and how can you build your toleration and acceptance of this position? How can you adapt to an understanding that other people are going to change; they are always in flow. Just because we're close doesn't mean we're the same or don't have differences. Just because we're close doesn't mean that this is going to shift any minute now. We can be close to others and separate from others. It's going to be both/and. Regardless of how much another threatens you, wills you, manipulates you, seduces you to stay close, there will always be an innate pull that gives us distance *and* closeness.

Chapter 17
Avoid Thinking in Terms of Good or Bad

Since the beginning of time, our frame has been to see things as either good or bad. Two little buckets, a little simple binary system of filing, good/bad, right/wrong, or good/evil—however you want to see it.

To practice expanding our vision means taking down that frame of "either/or." Literally taking down the frame so whatever we see is now seen from a frame of being neither good nor bad. It is both/and. There's nothing in the universe that's not both/and.

The universe is a spectrum of polarities, good and bad, alpha and omega. Until I can see it from that frame, I'm going to be victim to the bad, addicted to the good. Seeking, desiring, selling my soul for the good and affronted, afraid, panicked, and terrorized by the bad.

To the degree we can see the full spectrum, we can look at what's going on in our organizations, our relationships—in any situation—as neither good nor bad. We see through a frame that says, "Reality. This is the way of it," and that frame is both/and, not one or the other.

Chapter 17

It is what it is. What is, *is*, which leaves us more able to cope, to strategize, to think, to resource, to create, to innovate, to be thoughtful, calmer, take pauses, and to be generally less reactive to whatever's happening. When we no longer see events as either good or bad, we can see them as part of reality. Whatever it is, is going to shift anyway, just like the wind blows.

Chapter 18
How I Contributed to the Problem

I've not met many people who really like admitting they have contributed to upsets, or concerns, or what went down, or what didn't work out right, or whatever. I, on the other hand, have had a tendency to take responsibility for *everything* that happens, even when it's not my responsibility. In a grocery store aisle another shopper once bumped her cart into mine, and *I* apologized.

It's a fine line to look at how we contribute to problems without turning the situation back on ourselves to say that it was our fault, to believe we *caused* the situation. In this practice, we examine if in some way we have taken responsibility for people's actions, behaviors, and reactions that honestly have nothing to do with us.

Me, Saint Martha? No way. This is their problem, they don't understand, they need to do that, they should do this, if only, if only. When I come down off my high horse, I can then ask, *how did I contribute to the problem*, not *did I, how* did I do it? What role did I have in the situation? Where did I withhold? Where did I push? Where did I use force, where did I seduce, where did I manipulate?

Not, "*Do* I do these things? Yes, *where* do I do this; what is my role in the problem? All the power in the universe again is right there in that realization. When we wake up to 'this is my role in the situation,' we can clearly see the one place in the whole scene where we can change *anything*.

We can see how we contributed.

In some cases, it could be that we provoked in some way. It could be that when we don't get our way, we withhold love or attention. It may mean that when another person doesn't go along with us, we don't speak to them. If we don't feel supported in what we're doing, maybe we go silent, get quiet, shut down.

Years ago, I went away with friends for Labor Day weekend. One of the people on the trip had not told their family when they were going to be home. When we got home from the holiday and arrived at that friend's home, their spouse was so mad they couldn't talk. Nobody was speaking. It was a very awkward, very intense energy.

I stepped in and I took responsibility. I made myself responsible for the fact that my friend's spouse was mad at her – because she hadn't been home when her family expected her to be home.

To my best recall, that's the last time I actually did that.

Now, I look at a situation like this and think, "Ah, it's not my responsibility to communicate with her husband. It's not my responsibility to notify her family when we're going to be home. It's only my responsibility to notify people when I'm going to be home—and maybe not even then. It's my responsibility to communicate and do whatever I said I would do, and to make things right when I'm not able to do what I said I would do."

We contribute to a problem when we take the blame and make ourselves responsible if somebody else has a hurt feeling, or things don't go as they planned or they are experiencing edginess or upsets or whatever.

I've been working at this for years, to leave the problem between the true parties, to leave them responsible for themselves. Not to leave the people. But to leave the *responsibility* with them—where it belongs.

Look at your patterned ways of being and the effects of those patterns on your important relationships. Look at the effects on the dynamics of the relationship, and then on the dynamics of the way you function as a team, the way you function as an organization, the way you function as a family.

Ask yourself: What is my part in this interaction? That's the place you can make change. That's the place you can bring healing. That's the place you can restore yourself and open a field of infinite possibility. Instead of, "I don't have a part in this," or seeing it as, "I've been victimized again," remind yourself that there is no victim here. Look at what's your part in the situation. Change what you can, accept what you cannot change, and have a clear understanding of the difference between what you can and cannot change.

Chapter 19

Accept That Pain, Tension and Suffering Are Part of the Human Learning System

My least favorite principle is accepting that pain, tension, and suffering are part of the human learning system.

Who wants people to suffer? Not me. No sane person would want another human being to suffer. No sane parent would want their child to suffer. However, suffering is a part of being human. Tension, anxiety, disease, divorce, things that cause suffering—they are part of the human phenomena? Since recorded history, these incidents have been part of the human process of learning.

Maybe you want to wave a wand and magically remove all of the world's suffering. I believe that's why some of us are called to do the work we do. We actually believe we can stop suffering or remove it from out of the world somehow. Look at how the act of making suffering wrong or bad inhibits us, shuts us down, and closes the field of possibility.

Or maybe we believe we're victims of suffering. So we teach the world ways to avoid suffering. As if that's possible!

Welcome to reality. Welcome to the world. There's suffering here. Sometimes we get what we want, sometimes we don't get what we want. Sometimes we have long periods of illness and disease. We have marriages and births, deaths and divorces. It's all part of the spectrum of being a human being.

We can approach pain, tension, and suffering with an attitude that "something's been done to me" or "I'm a victim to this," *or* we can approach such events as "This is a part of the human learning process."

If I could wrap a prayer around this tenet, it would be: "Life, please help us accept this learning process as a very real part of our humanity. And spare me from believing there's anything about suffering that can be avoided, and accept that suffering comes in the doses it comes in, in the amount that it comes in, and I don't get to choose."

When my dad was ill, he needed physical therapy, occupational therapy, and speech therapy—all at the same time. On the bottom of one heel, he had weakness and a large ulcer. According to him—even with all the other pain and surgeries and suffering, cancers, bleeding ulcers, collapsed lungs and everything else he had going on—these raw nerve endings on the bottom of this foot was the most intense, unbearable pain he had ever felt. Each time he was in the hospital, with more critical issues to tend to, the sore on his foot would often be overlooked, getting worse as he lay in the bed, with his full pressure on his heel.

I had watched him groan and grimace and suffer through so many seemingly larger issues—trying to swallow, learning to speak again after radiation and chemo treatments, and now here he was in physical therapy, so weak he couldn't lift his legs. It was so very tempting to walk over and lift his legs for him, to do the physical therapy motions and movements *for* him. I found myself having to *grow myself up* until I was able to watch him stumble, suffer a fall, fail time and time again. All of which was required for him to get his *own* orientation and capacities for walking again, standing, and healing.

Learning to let others experience their process around pain and tension and suffering has been one of the hardest things I've done—not just with my dad, but with all people.

In one of the workshops I teach, we evaluate healthy helping and a specific tendency we "highly-responsible" types have in this area. We often have a high level of pain tolerance in ourselves *and* we often have a very low tolerance of pain in other people. The second someone else has any suffering, we swoop in. I'm prone to this, to rescue others from these situations, to fix it, make it all right, ease it, take responsibility for it. How about you?

Certainly, compassion fatigue, burnout, codependency, enmeshment, and every other similar problematic issue arises out of not being able to bear or build stamina for another person's pain and suffering. It's a practice to accept that human beings are going to have tension, anxiety, suffering, physical pain, diseases, illnesses, ailments, broken bones, recovery, loss, and everything else throughout the spectrum.

We don't have to love or even like that these incidents occur. Our practice is to simply accept this part of being human, which has been in existence since the creation of time. The pain is inevitable; the suffering is more optional. When we can witness another's suffering and not join it, then we don't add to suffering in the world.

Chapter 19

We're not the director of the universe. Shocker. And if we put ourselves in that position as the director of the universe, then we're going to live our lives very irritated, frustrated, and angry at the suffering in the world, versus doing what we can to end the suffering in the world.

Which means we start by ending the suffering that is here in our presence, and *then* be a space for other people who are suffering. Until we can end *our* suffering and *our* resistance to suffering, there's no possibility we can end it in the world.

To accept that suffering, tension, anxiety, and conflict are parts of the human learning process—whether we like it or not—that's the way of it.

Coffee Break

You're ALMOST there! This is further than most people make it through most books, so you deserve a little break and some encouragement. Grab your drink of choice and soak in this wisdom:

"Whatever I'm observing or judging is an aspect of myself."

"Drop the belief that I'm going to get what I want."

"When I notice I am in emotional hell hotel — Remember -- I've got the key. I can check out anytime I want."

"Lead me not into the temptation of my mind, patterns and burdened parts of myself. Deliver me from the error of my thinking."

Chapter 20
Cultivate Your Own Imagination

The most common use of imagination is worry, fear, scaring, or outright terrorizing ourselves by imaging a future we don't want. We tend to imagine bad things happening in the future.

Cultivating imagination in the direction of what is possible is a helpful process for harnessing creativity. Working with a *can-do* attitude, imagining what positive outcomes are possible in any situation, carries a causative, creative energy for me. This is how naturally imagination can be used *for* something, rather than *against* it.

Instead of being focused on a condition or a circumstance, it's time to cultivate your own imagination. Imagine for yourself, "What else is possible here? In this very situation, what else is possible?" Every speck of technology, innovation, and creation has been born out of this practice.

We get to discover how to be imaginative in a state of creation. This helps us move away from the fearful, horror-movie state and into a state of "What else is possible? What would happen if I did this?"

This is a Thomas Edison kind of imagination. "What would happen here? What happens if I do this? What happens if do that? Wearing the hat of a researcher, let me test this."

Cultivating how to be more imaginative from a point of creation, from a point of innovation, allows our dreaming and thinking to be more grounded and rooted in the power of an imagination to create something as yet unseen. To create something the world could, would, maybe will even laugh at. And to keep our capacity for creation and our capability to imagine, even if they do.

The way I understand it, we're the only species with the capacity to actually imagine and to use imagination as a force to create.

What are you doing in your life right now, and what *can* you do in your life, to cultivate your own imagination and your own imaginative capacities in the ways you lead? How can you think more broadly than even what we've been able to discover in this book, in the ways you lead, parent, in your marriage and other relationships? How can you be innovative and creative even in the relationships you already have?

From the time we first were able to play, dream, make believe—all the way up to the grave—our imagination is intact and operating and available to us.

Approaching imagination this way, we can ask ourselves creative, appreciative questions: *What could become of this? How could this be a good thing? If the universe is friendly, then how can I use this for my own salvation, for my own awakening, for my own sake?*

By answering these questions, with the power of imagining providing just a peek into another possibility for ourselves, we can use this power as a creative, causative force.

Chapter 21
Hang in There

The human spirit is one of the things that inspires me the most to continue to do the work I do. I'm blown away constantly by the spirit of human beings, and what we can bear, what we can experience, what we can heal from, what we can resolve, and move through. It fascinates me that we are wired for this forbearance.

We have a built-in, uncommon motivation, perseverance, resilience, and ability to look back when something presents itself, and to say, "How did I do this before? How did I grow through this before?" We harbor a capacity in ourselves to say, "I am equipped for this regardless of what's presenting in my life." A circumstance may look like it's insurmountable. That we can't do what we are being called to do. This is the salute of the victim: "Oh, I can't."

Even with the pressure and the temptation to salute our circumstances as a victim, crying out "why me? " we can take a position of resilience.

Decide for yourself, *I can*. Then ask, *How can I? What's possible here?* This is *also* hard-wired and innate in us; this uncommon motivation to try something different, pick ourselves up, brush ourselves off, and get back at it, knowing that the universal life force is what is sourcing us.

How do we become aware of something greater than ourselves in the times when we lose motivation or lose our theme, lose our certainty or our faith that we can do this? How do we tap into something greater than this to pick ourselves back up and persevere even when it doesn't make sense to do so?

To me, this practice of *Hang in There* translates to being uncommonly motivated to see something through. There have been many times I drew on an uncommon motivation to see things through when I didn't feel alive in the activity. For me, getting back in touch with the *why* of what I'm doing, makes it absolutely possible.

My completing this book is the greatest example. I've been working with this material for decades now. I love the material; I love the work. I shared this work in a video series. A gracious friend videotaped me and we made the tapes into a series. This friend did these videos primarily on her own accord, out of her generosity and her appreciation for the work.

Then the video series was discovered and found. It went straight to the globally-streaming New Thought Channel for all the world to see. Thousands of people joined in, viewed the series, and benefited from it. One executive at the company thought the material was so good it ought to be put in a book, and encouraged me to head in that direction. I said yes to it, even though I didn't really have the motivation to do any more work on it than I had already done.

We transcribed the material and it felt like this book was nearly ready. All the book needed was a few more add-ons from me, a few more examples of how I practice this in my daily life. In that moment, this uncommon motivation kicked in for me to pull the material up again, look at it, remember how much I love it, how much I want this teaching out in the world.

My vision is to get this teaching to the whole of humanity. And when I get back in touch with my *why*—the reason I'm doing this, and what it's for—a new vitality, new resurgence of energy, and new passion are all activated in me. Right then and there, I sat my butt down in a chair, carved out several hours and recorded the additional material for all the chapters in this book so we can get this book out into the world.

These teachings could be limited, and yet they are *not* limited, because of the act of perseverance, the process of simply hanging in there. I trust that your reading this book right now is the manifestation of me reaching as broadly as I can. As we both put these processes into action in our lives, together we reach broader into humanity. Together we can do what any one of us cannot do alone.

Chapter 22
Be Willing to Learn

I am a lifelong student. I've got all sorts of credentials, certifications, and degrees. I've got three or four degrees and an equal number of ordinations, all from my love of learning. Being willing to learn comes easily to me in most areas of my life.

Where I'm *not willing* to learn, however, has been some of the most painful arenas in my life. I accept that learning is part of the process. I also accept that *not* being willing to learn—not having the stamina or interest to learn or even open my mind to something new at times—is *also* part of my own humanity.

Be willing to be challenged by life. Be willing to see life and appreciate life as a mystery, even as a puzzle. Approach life's situations as a puzzle: "How can I put these pieces in place?" Be intrigued by life; approach it from a mindset of curiosity.

Life's not designed to be understood, organized, or ordered. Life's not designed to work with us getting all these ducks in a row. Mystery of the Universe? Planets in alignment? Planets suspended in space, spinning this way, then spinning this way, and then that way? How can we be in the mystery of life, learning from it and intrigued by it? How can we approach each situation, each relationship?

Be curious about what's possible. Be intrigued by life. Be challenged by it in a good way, living from a "What's possible?" perspective, rather than "It's been done to me again," perspective.

Being willing to learn still motivates me. The drive in me to gain knowledge, and to apply that knowledge, is unparalleled to any other desire in me. A coach told me many years ago that I had a core belief that *I don't know*—and that *not knowing* was like a cross I bore. I worked with this concept for several years as though uncovering a curse of some sort, behind this core, deep-seeded belief of *I don't know*.

In the process, I discovered that not knowing keeps me reading books, taking workshops, attending seminars, signing up for programs, teaching workshops and seminars, and growing and stretching myself to learn new ways of being and doing in the world.

Over time, I realized that *I don't know* is my only reality. The difference between feeling this as a burden and recognizing it as my reality is stark and profound. *I don't know*. And I don't mind that I don't know.

Now, my willingness to learn has more peace about it. I don't pressure myself as much as in years past, *and* I'm still very motivated to learn and to be willing to learn without so much effort.

Chapter 23
Have a Clear Vision

Before you make your bed, you have a clear vision about how you want the bed to look. If you're going to paint something, you already have something in mind. Most of us wouldn't start painting without having some kind of outcome in mind. Having a clear vision of a project provides sanity and solid ground.

Do you have a clear vision for life's situations? It can be something as simple as "What do I really want to do in this situation? Not "what should I do for others," but "what interests me in this situation? What clear vision am I holding for an outcome? What's a clear vision of what's possible here?"

Having a clear vision, for me, means looking at what I'm doing. Asking myself *what for*—uncovering the *why* of what I'm doing, and the *what* that's motivating me to do it. "What do I think the outcomes will get me? What will be the cost of doing it? What will I have to set aside to do it? Am I going to look back on my life, reflect on my life, and be proud that I did this, happy that I did this, or look back on my life and wish that I hadn't done what I've done?"

In the past, having a clear vision of my life required me to pause, practice purification to set aside old beliefs, and break out of old patterns. I invested time to *really* question *who* and *what* I wanted to be in the world, to see what legacy I want to leave, and to recognize which goals I have for my life that are actual and true and which are adopted or adapted, handed down through my family, for example. I used the pause to make decisions that moved me in the direction of what was true for me.

I no longer wait for a clearer vision. When I have a vision, even if it seems confusing or not yet settled, I'm not as demanding that it be crystal-clear. I don't put my foot down, declaring I'm not going to move toward my vision until it is completely clear, until all the channels are opened.

In the past, my process looked like *I want to go to Dallas and I'm not going to go to Dallas until all the traffic lights are green between here and Dallas.* Well then, I'm never even going to start for Dallas, am I? These days, my process is more flexible, more open: *I'm going to start for Dallas, and I'll deal with the traffic lights as I get to them. I know some will be green and some may not;* and *that's not fatal.*

Be willing for a vision to be as clear as it is and or get clearer over time. Keep your eyes on the vision and keep going in that direction. Be aware that you're well-equipped and fully supported in navigating any of the winds between point A and point B as you move in the direction of your vision.

Chapter 24
Develop a Wide Repertoire of Responses

I've noticed that we're patterned to respond to situations in our lives less with responses and more with reactions—very much like animals. We seem to have a limited repertoire of *fight, flight, and freeze*, with many different flavors of those three.

To mature, to become higher, to get more equipped in responding rather that reacting, we need a more innovative response than these knee-jerk instinctual reactivities.

Especially when it comes to anger. I don't know about you, but I want to be able to respond to anger more broadly than I have in the past.

When it comes to our responses, we're patterned. We typically run on two or three tracks. We're predictable. People know where our buttons are. They know when they push the button, generally, how we're going to react. The practice of developing a wider repertoire of response is an unwiring of those buttons. We may still have the buttons, but now they're deactivated.

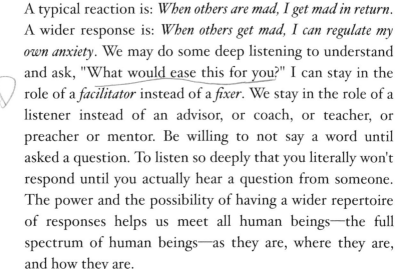

A typical reaction is: *When others are mad, I get mad in return.* A wider response is: *When others get mad, I can regulate my own anxiety.* We may do some deep listening to understand and ask, "What would ease this for you?" I can stay in the role of a *facilitator* instead of a *fixer.* We stay in the role of a listener instead of an advisor, or coach, or teacher, or preacher or mentor. Be willing to not say a word until asked a question. To listen so deeply that you literally won't respond until you actually hear a question from someone. The power and the possibility of having a wider repertoire of responses helps us meet all human beings—the full spectrum of human beings—as they are, where they are, and how they are.

So how can we develop a broader response so we don't always react with the same, knee-jerk reaction? If we're going to tackle just anger, for example, how can we consciously, purposefully, intentionally build a repertoire of response that will move us out of this knee-jerk patterned way of responding?

Now, if you start doing this in your household, or in your organization, with your board of directors, they'll think you're on a new medication—because we've taught them where our buttons are. We've taught them how we're going to respond. We've taught them our knee-jerk reaction. When we start to deactivate some of these buttons, it can be very disorienting to others. As you're building this practice, be aware that it can be disorienting to the people around you, and they may resist. Stay the course.

According to the theory, anytime we make any hint of a change in a situation, the system puts pressure on us to change back. When we can hold a higher note, so to speak, over time the system recalibrates. The system itself can then come to a higher note, higher consciousness, higher thinking. The system begins to recognize a world of more possibility and less restriction. Expect some resistance when you start to do this work, and stay the course. There's a lot of support for you.

Chapter 25
Allow Time for Things to Process

Allow time? Ugh! For me, allowing time meant take a minute. Wail, pray, get over it. Make amends, say you're sorry, let's get on with it.

How intolerant and arrogant I was, trying to rush the human process, trying to rush emotional processes. My innocent and very naïve quick-fix mentality was that we can hurry through pain, or rush past discomfort, instead of allowing time.

Just like a fever, events in our lives take the time they need to burn off. The process could last weeks, months, years, or even decades for some. We don't get to pick how quickly something is moved through us, how quickly something is healed or how quickly something is understood.

It's ineffective for us as leaders to think we can rush a process or not be more patient. Be tolerant, accepting, and strategic in allowing time, whatever amount it is, to pass.

I can report that I've matured a little. From my early internal unfavorable reaction, I'm just a hair above it now.

Chapter 25

I'm less surprised at how long it takes for somebody to heal, to move through something and to resolve something. What I know for sure is that timing is none of my business. My patience, how I accept what I cannot change, *is* my business—and operating from that awareness is often a full-time job for me.

Chapter 26
Accept Solitude

Sometimes, we're going to stand alone. Others won't understand us. It may appear that others are not there for us; they don't support us, they're against us. This is where the practice of accepting solitude comes into play. To take time away to think, to get clear about who you are, who you've come here to be. To think about what is yours to do, and what is not yours to do.

What is your responsibility and what is not your responsibility? Take time, be quiet, use prayer, fasting, restoration, silence, reflection, and reading. Whatever helps you *remember* you. Some way for you to remember what is true for you and what is not. Take time in solitude. Not solitude in reaction, of like, "I'm out of here!" but solitude that's purposeful and intentional, that says, "I need to clear my own mind. I need to get clearer about my own thinking. I need to clarify what I will do and won't do. I need to clarify it through my best thinking, not emotional reactivity, until I see what possibilities exist for me."

My need and desire and responsibility for solitude is one of the most important things to me in my personal life and in my profession. I *take* solitude. Truly take it. For the past 40 years, I have scheduled myself off the grid, so to speak—without technology, newspapers, the outside world—for ten-day periods at a time. I engage in deep meditative practices, such as Vipassana meditation, ten days of silence and *noble silence* where you actually don't look anyone in the eye or read or engage in anything other than meditation in times of silence and solitude. No talking whatsoever. I've taken mystery-school initiations and rituals. I've gifted myself with ten days of sequestering myself to rest and restore.

In my twenties, I needed so much time for solitude—and I couldn't see a place for it in my busy life. Luckily, people assumed—because of how busy I was during the week—that I would be just as busy on the weekends. I used these assumptions to my advantage and took one weekend a month alone and in silence. I believe this practice allowed me to keep myself together during some of those intense times when I was working so many jobs and going to college full-time. This solitary practice made it possible for me to use the bandwidth I possessed then. Having designated times of solitude is what makes it possible for me to run the bandwidth that I still do now, forty years later.

Creating solitude has meant doing some very courageous and often uncomfortable things—like saying *no* to having a roommate, sharing hotel rooms, or even sharing my bed. It means saying *yes* to taking trips by myself, eating meals by myself in silence, and sequestering myself.

Some people are not wired this way. They find it shocking or even scary when someone wants or needs the kind of solitary time I create for myself. For me, solitude frees— and gives me strength, vitality, renewal, restoration. The same time in solitude could very well put someone else in a psych ward. There is no formula for solitude. As much as I need it and depend on it, to some degree solitude is not for everybody.

To accept solitude in your life means not pushing against solitude. Many people want the benefit of solitude, but their self-talk is so strong, they can't even be alone with their own thoughts. Practice being in a room without distractions or background noise. Practice accepting the everyday solitude that occurs in your life without filling up that space.

Afterword

Whew! We've made it through twenty-six possibilities for presence, and I invite you to start with a devoted practice of applying one or more. Practically apply these principles and see what possibilities you experience in your own life.

If I had to make a summary statement about this book, I'd tell you it's designed to help you become a well-differentiated, mature person; a stronger leader in your life.

To become well-differentiated and mature, we have to focus on our own functioning, while staying in relationship with others. One must think from the "I" position, not the "they" position. The "I" position. Self-differentiation is indeed good stewardship of the self.

Don't just believe me; don't just take my word. Try this on for yourself, see what's possible. If you've got questions, or want to contact me directly, you can reach me at marthacreek.com.

When it comes to effective leadership, what I know for sure, for me, is that I cannot be spiritually mature without being emotionally mature. This self-differentiated work is a life's work. It's not a quick fix. It's not a "tick-box" exercise.

I honor the fact that you will read here, learn here, and then put this out in the world through your own experiences, through living it out in your own life. I send you the richest, most heartfelt blessings, as you continue to do your work. If there's a way I can support you, it's yours.

Explore the full video series on Presence and Functioning on Youtube:
https://youtu.be/IN8h2iuu5fI?si=osGDXv-QRNNAAcLm

Also by Martha Creek

Wisdom *pours* forth through these grassroots anecdotes from a myriad of topics. Enjoy an uplift in your spiritual practices of gratitude, empowered teaching, forgiveness, goal setting, spark and purpose, intentions, prayer, faith, and imagination.

Gain insight and perspective on the potential and power of doing small things in great ways in all areas of your life.

This writing speaks to the ***full spectrum of our humanness***, integrated *gracefully* and *mercifully* in divinity. You may actually learn something, better yet ***re-learn*** something and at a minimum just simply feel better from knowing there is "another way" of being.

Get **Martha's Pearls** in digital, paperback, or color paperback.

About the Author

Widely known in New Thought communities, Rev. Dr. Martha Creek's empowered trainings approach deep inner-work as a courageous adventurer. A master of the art of right questioning, she calls forth the patterns to create a new way of being, literally. She is available for guest speaking, keynotes, workshops, seminars, team building and development, and personal coaching.

www.MarthaCreek.com

Ordained in Religious Science and Divine Science, Martha has served as Great Lakes Unity Consultant, a member of Unity Institute faculty, and is a member of the Affiliated New Thought Network (ANTN). She has attended Emerson Theological Seminary (Masters and Doctorate), Byron Katie School for *The Work*, and Hoffman Institute. She is a Healthy Congregations Facilitator and Trainer. Martha is committed to get empowered teachings to the whole of the planet. Her mission is simple and profound, "to serve those who serve."

Made in the USA
Monee, IL
19 October 2023

44830548R00077